Touching the Truth

A Summary and Commentary on
The Splendor of Truth

the Tenth Encyclical Letter
of Pope John Paul II

by

Rev. William N. Seifert, M. Div.
William F. Urbine, M.A., M.Ed., D. Min.
and Rev. Michael P. Orsi, M. Div., Ed. D.

Foreword by
Most Rev. James T. McHugh
Bishop of Camden

ST. PAUL BOOKS & MEDIA

Imprimatur:
Most Rev. Thomas J. Welsh
Bishop of Allentown
February 18, 1994

ISBN 0-8198-7379-9

Printed and published in the U.S.A. by St. Paul Books & Media, 50 St. Paul's Avenue, Boston, MA 02130

St. Paul Books & Media is the publishing house of the Daughters of St. Paul, an international congregation of women religious serving the Church with the communications media.

1 2 3 4 5 6 7 8 9 99 98 97 96 95 94

Contents

A Prayer for the Guidance of the Mother of God

O Mary

Mother of Mercy, watch over all people, that the cross of Christ may not be emptied of its power, that man may not stray from the path of the good or become blind to sin, but may put his hope ever more fully in God, who is "rich in mercy" (Eph 2:4).

May we carry out the good works prepared by God beforehand (cf. Eph 2:10) and so live completely "for the praise of his glory" (Eph 1:12).

VS n.120

Foreword

On October 5, 1993, Pope John Paul II issued *The Splendor of Truth*, an encyclical letter on Catholic moral teaching. In this document the Holy Father intends to set forth the principles of a moral teaching based upon Sacred Scripture and the living Apostolic Tradition and at the same time to shed light on the presuppositions and consequences of the dissent which that teaching has met.

The encyclical is timely in that it addresses the moral crisis of our times. As evidenced by a number of recent books here in the United States, efforts to reduce religion to a matter of private choice have diminished its force in setting an overall moral tone for society. Crime, violence, drug abuse and out-of-wedlock pregnancy are some of the consequences resulting from the absence of generally accepted moral or ethical principles. Many of our social commentators tell us that an over-emphasis on individualism to the neglect of the common good has eroded our capacity to live in harmony, peace and mutual respect. When individual choice and unlimited freedom are the prevailing norms, the only law is the law of the jungle—the survival of the fittest.

The Splendor of Truth confronts the morally pathological atmosphere of modern society. It emphasizes the common good, the need for social justice and social responsibility and the importance of the natural law as a foundation of moral doctrine.

The encyclical, responding to the direction of the Second Vatican Council, invokes the teaching of Sacred Scripture—both Old and New Testament. But the primary moral teacher is Jesus Christ, and his moral teaching is the inspiration and direction for Catholic moral theology. The entire first part of the encyclical focuses on each person's relationship with God through Jesus Christ, and the salvific nature of Christ's teaching and example. Christ himself taught that salvation is secured by obeying "the commandments of Sinai" and following the Sermon on the Mount, "the magna charta of Gospel morality."

The Splendor of Truth argues that objective morality is necessary not only for personal perfection but also to assure order in society. At the same time, it affirms the importance of conscience, a conscience formed on truth and the radical freedom to follow God's law.

The encyclical also upholds the objective morality of norms that specify the good or malice of human acts. While personal intention and the circumstances surrounding an action are important, primary consideration is given to the inherent purpose of the act itself. Some actions are intrinsically evil because, by their nature, they contradict God's plan or are inherently opposed to truth or the dignity, integrity and vocation of the human person (cf. *Gaudium et Spes*, 27).

The Splendor of Truth provides new insights on the relationship of truth, freedom and moral good. It rejects the separation of morality from faith or religious conversion and commitment. Such separation is all too often the case under modern secularism. The encyclical also affirms the need for courage and heroism in living the moral ideal, a heroism that in some cases may lead to martyrdom.

John Paul II calls on moral theologians to pursue their work in union with and at the service of the Church. This means acknowledgement of the uniqueness of the Church's teaching office as fulfilled by the Pope and the bishops, and service to the people of God by assisting them in their efforts to live morally good lives. It also means a positive and open cooperation with the Church's magisterium. *The Splendor of Truth* distinguishes moral theology, which has a normative dimension, from the behavioral and social sciences, which are more descriptive and interpretive. In this regard it is important to realize that moral norms are based on objective values and universal principles, not on opinion polls or public consensus.

The encyclical rejects prolonged and systematic dissent, which is opposed to ecclesial communion, contrary to a correct understanding of the structure and teaching office of the Church, and a threat to the right of the faithful to receive Catholic doctrine in its purity and integrity.

A final section of the encyclical calls upon bishops to fulfill their role as moral teachers. This involves awareness of their teaching responsibility, their pastoral role and their obligation to safeguard and proclaim Catholic teaching faithfully and courageously. Bishops should provide clear direction to priests and call upon them as a presbyterate, to complement the bishop's teaching role. In a special way bishops should see to it that organizations and agencies that call themselves Catholic are in fact faithful to the Church's mission and teaching.

The Splendor of Truth is a valuable contemporary document that is intended to assist bishops and priests in their moral teaching and counselling. It is a courageous document, in that it confronts many contemporary errors and trends. It will be of immense value in the training of priests and religious and lay leaders, so that they in turn may help people distinguish good from evil and pursue their God-given vocation to come to the fullness of life in Jesus Christ. This popular presentation by Father William Seifert, Dr. William Urbine and Father Michael Orsi provides an accurate and succinct rendering of the major theses of *The Splendor of Truth*. It will be immensely helpful to teachers and their students in understanding John Paul II's reflection on the Church's contemporary role as moral teacher, and our universal responsibility to not only live good moral lives, but at the same time to pursue a deeper personal unity with Christ, the source and center of the Christian life.

Most Reverend James T. McHugh, D.D., S.T.D.
Bishop of Camden
January 10, 1994

Introductory Essay

Why an Encyclical?

Papal encyclicals can be understood as "the nearest thing to an authentic synthesis of the Catholic view."[1] Statements are issued by specific *popes*, and the coherence of the body of encyclicals can be understood to reflect the integrity of Church teaching. As such, the contents of any one encyclical, let alone all the encyclicals of any pontificate, or a series of encyclicals over the years, becomes a means through which the integrity of Catholic teaching can be set forth.[2] These teachings are often presented to correct errors that emerge within a given age and are read fruitfully in the light of specific controversies.

The encyclicals of Pope John Paul II set a theological trajectory rising from his vision of the unalienable dignity of the human person. This trajectory incorporates the role of the family, the importance of culture, the economic and political orders and other striking points.[3] *Veritatis Splendor* sets forth, for the first time in such a detailed form, the basic elements of

1. Anne Fremantle, *The Papal Encyclicals* (New York: Mentor Press, 1956), 9.
2. Michael J. Shuck, *That They Be One: the social teaching of the papal encyclicals, 1740-1898* (Washington, D.C.: Georgetown University Press, 1991), 45.
3. Dulles, Avery, "The Prophetic Humanism of Pope John Paul II," *America* 169, No. 12 (Oct. 23, 1993): 6-11.

that teaching necessary to present universal moral principles across cultures and pastoral circumstances (cf. *VS n.* 114).

The Church has always taught that certain kinds of actions are intrinsically evil. Pope Paul VI taught in *Humanae Vitae* that contraception fell into this category. Some theologians rejected his teaching. Some dissenters were in need of a theory to justify themselves and turned to a theory that said no specific kind of action is intrinsically evil, anything can be sometimes right and any commandment is open to exception. These theologians said there can be circumstances in which a normally forbidden action represents a lesser evil and there can be a proportionate reason to do it. The theory has its philosophical roots in utilitarianism, pragmatism and majoritarianism, which admit to no moral absolute other than the good being determined by the outcome or the greatest benefit for the greatest number. Building on these philosophies, Joseph Fletcher presented a theology known as situation ethics. This served as a foundation for later consequentialist and proportionalist theologians. It is against this philosophical and theological mentality that the Holy Father takes aim in this encyclical.

The Christological Context

The Christological context of the encyclical presents its basic theme: "a call to live in Christ, who alone reveals man's highest calling." *Veritatis Splendor* shows Christ to be more than a lawgiver and teacher. It proclaims Christ as the God-man who shows himself to be the norm of what it means to be truly human. Christian morality, according to the Pope, is richer than a mere scientific knowledge of moral propositions. Rather, it is living in Christ. This is, as the Holy Father writes in the encyclical: *...a lived knowledge of Christ, a living remembrance of his commandments and a truth to be lived out...a decision involving one's whole existence* (*VS*, *n.* 88).

The Link with Ecclesiology

Throughout the past century substantial questions have been raised against the horizon of Church teachings. The advance of historical-critical methods led some scholars to question the very foundations of the Christian faith. As a result, there seems to be a general yet systematic calling into question of traditional moral doctrine on the basis of anthropological and ethical concepts. Moral reflection continues to develop as the Christian community is challenged by new situations. Therefore it is necessary to clarify the points of doctrine that are crucial for resolution of this crisis (*nn.* 10-12). Through the writings and addresses of the *popes* from Leo XXIII to John Paul II, these public and lasting documents seek to fulfill the Lord's command given at the birth of his Church.[4]

The Link with Evangelization

Evangelization is intrinsic to the nature and life of the Church.[5] Begun by the mandate of Jesus himself, and continued under the authority of the Holy Spirit, the spread of the Gospel has advanced throughout history and has touched all human cultures. The crisis of dechristianization, evident in the patterns of behavior and divergent visions of the human person in the present age, prompts the response of reaffirming the truth of the saving mystery of the redemption by Jesus Christ.

Modern thought ultimately separates the exercise of human freedom from its essential and constructive relationship with truth. Autonomous reason (quite isolated from revelation, tradition and the Magisterium and even from our antecedent truth) is being used to establish norms relative to the "human good." This autonomy has called into question the intrinsic connection between faith and morality. Faith is not merely an

---

4. Cf. John 15.
5. See *Evangelii Nuntiandi* and *Catechesi Tradendae.*

intellectual consent to certain abstract truths; it also possesses a moral content. Faith calls forth a consistent life commitment. It entails and brings to perfection the keeping of the commandments. At the heart of this message is the conviction that only in the truth does man's freedom become truly human and responsible (nn.36, 40).

It is the task of all the Christian faithful—laity and clergy alike—to proclaim the Gospel to all nations. *Veritatis Splendor* sets before the world a clear and priceless vision of the splendor of the Truth that is revealed in Jesus Christ. It is this Truth that is proclaimed by his Church. It is the call to conversion that stands at the heart of this encyclical. In his apostolic exhortation *Christifidelis Laici*, Pope John Paul anticipates this theme. He notes:

> *Opening wide the doors to Christ, accepting him into humanity itself poses absolutely no threat to persons, indeed it is the only road to take to arrive at the total truth and the exalted value of the human individual* (n. 34).

Though somewhat difficult because of the method and terms used, studying this document as a work of faith will enrich the reader. Such study seems warranted in the face of the call to re-evangelize the world for Christ.

Critical Discernment of Certain Trends in Theology

Since the close of the Second Vatican Council a variety of "schools" of theological reflection have emerged. Representative of these are the Christian personalist, consequentialist and feminist theologies, liberation and the historical-conscious studies, natural moral law, neo-scholasticist, neo-thomist, proportionalist, revisionist and situationalist schools, and the theology of compromise. Some have laid claim to be a legitimate voice within the larger Catholic tradition. Others have clearly departed from the official teaching of the Catholic Church over specific moral interpretations of human acts and reflect the systematic dissent that has emerged over the past decades. The rejection of the natural moral law method as well as questions about the efficacy of universally valid moral norms served as the source for much of the conflict that arose as a result of theological dissent (cf. *VS* n. 4).

Fr. John Neuhaus notes, in a *Wall Street Journal* article:

> *Modernity...has been very big on freedom. But now freedom has been untethered from truth, and freedom cannot stand alone without degenerating into license. License, in turn, is the undoing of freedom, for then, as Nietzsche and others recognized, all personal and social life become simply the assertion of power.*
>
> *If freedom is to be secured, power—and freedom itself—must be accountable to truth. Or, as John Paul II puts it repeatedly, "Authentic freedom is ordered to truth."*

Given these developments in contemporary theology, John Paul II chose to use this teaching to reaffirm the place of natural law in doing theology.

Catholic Doctrine and the Place of Natural Law

Human freedom and God's law meet and intersect. The "natural law," the participation of God's eternal law in the rational creature, implies that reason and the moral precepts which derive from it are essentially subordinate to divine wisdom. In opposition to *relativism*, the precepts of this moral law possess a universal and permanent character. *Conscience* is not a tribunal which creates the good; conscience must be formed in the light of truth enlightened by the divine law, the universal and objective laws of morality. One's *fundamental option* is involved every time a person in conscience and free choice acts contrary to the Christian moral life where serious moral matter is concerned, which is to commit a *mortal sin*. The morality of an act depends on the object of choice; thus, certain kinds of behavior are opposed to the truth and the good of the person. *Teleological* ethical theories such as *proportionalism* and *consequentialism,* while acknowledging that moral values are indicated by reason and revelation, allege that it is never possible to formulate an absolute prohibition of particular kinds of behavior which would be in conflict in every circumstance and in every culture with those values. On the contrary, the Church teaches it is never licit even for the most grave reasons to do evil that good may come of it. There are certain moral precepts forbidding certain kinds of behavior that have universal value and are always without exception valid. (Please confer with the glossary on page 49 for definitions of the italicized terms found in the above text.)

Following is a summary of some current theological positions. These positions, popularized by the authors cited below, are most often the source of controversial approaches in moral theology.

Current Controversies Addressed

Source: Contextual Morality

Proposal: Moral norms are time conditioned and relevant only as moral exhortations. Ethical decisions must be based on natural law and the modern sciences.

A representative writer for this thesis is Fr. Richard McCormick, S.J.

Reply: Moral theology is theology only if based on God's word. Jesus provided principles by which the Church can apply God's plan. While the Bible confirms the commandments and other natural law norms, it also relates them to the Blessed Trinity, which as our goal is beyond the grasp of natural reason and which adds new obligations such as norms concerning the sacraments.

Source: Theology of Compromise

Proposal: The "theology of compromise" argues that some acts against natural law are objectively justified because in a fallen world it is not always possible to fulfill that law.

Fr. Charles Curran is the principal proponent of this position.

Reply: Objective acts against natural law are always harmful to our nature; even if we are ignorant or lack freedom, nature does not compromise.

Source: Historical Consciousness

Proposal: Shows human nature as always changing. The notion of "natural moral law" belongs to a classical-minded deductive method now obsolete.

Reply: Jesus implies a human nature common to all. Good philosophy and theology are both deductive and inductive.

Source: Physicalism

Proposal: The Magisterium is mistakenly physicalistic when it teaches that a good intention can be vitiated merely by a disordered external physical act—e.g., a homosexual act cannot express true and moral love.

Reply: Human acts have their source in their extended purpose. If we know the physical act to be disordered, the intention is itself disordered.

Source: Proportionalism

Proposal: The "principle of proportionate reason" states that negative moral norms admit exceptions when an act's pre-moral positive values exceed its pre-moral negative values.

Fr. Joseph Fuchs, SJ, is a key proponent of this system.

Reply: They propose to weigh merely the pre-moral values of an act—e.g., the act considered apart from relation to the goal of human life. There is no way to weigh these "values" by any morally relevant standard. This is irreconcilable with the Christian faith.

A "Restoration" of the Role of Assent

Another effect of the ensuing discord was the retrieval of the rightful place of theological assent among many faithful Catholics. The role of the theologian and the relationship of academic theology to the Magisterium needed clearer definition. Statements were issued under the authority of Popes Paul VI and John Paul II seeking to clarify the exact nature of the relationship. The revised codes of Latin and Oriental Law, the *Catechism of the Catholic Church* and this encyclical present responses to these questions. They are summarized in *Veritatis Splendor*:

Theology is at the service of the Church. The Church is called to witness and evangelize the faith.

The task of teaching the Truth of the faith to the faithful is properly that of the legitimate pastors and those mandated by them for that purpose.

The need for a normative ground for moral judgment calls for the restoration of the vision of a loyal assent in dogmatic and moral theology (cf. *VS* n.109).

The Scripture-Grounded Revision of Moral Theology

The need for a clear revision of moral theology led many to question an exclusively philosophical basis for doing moral theology. This encyclical explains the biblical foundations, the ethical significance and the anthropological concerns undergirding the moral doctrine and vision of man set forth by the Church (cf. *VS* n.110). It solidly reaffirms the natural moral tradition, and in doing so, it sets the proper horizon for accurate and solid theological development into the third millennium of Christianity. The encyclical lays new ground integrating modern biblical scholarship with patristic exegetical methodology within a substantial personalist reflection. The patristic tradition of exegesis used by the Pope allows for a particular scripture passage to be open for any particular interpretation on an allegorical basis. Hence, the Pope uses the story of the rich young man for pastoral and pedagogical purposes presenting the challenge of authentic discipleship as both a moral and a doctrinal issue. This method first appeared in the "Wednesday catechesis" of Pope John Paul II, where this method of analysis is explained and used extensively.[6]

The Relationship to the New Catechism

Until 1993, many of the faithful awaited some revision of the Roman Catechism. A new catechism—the *Catechism of the Catholic Church*— was promulgated by the Holy See in

---

6. The following sources make available this catechesis, should a more detailed study of the method be desired: Pope John Paul II. *Blessed are the Pure of Heart: Catechesis on the Sermon on the Mount and Writings of St Paul.* Boston, MA, Daughters of St. Paul, © 1983; *Reflections on Humanae Vitae: Conjugal Morality and Spirituality.* Boston, MA, Daughters of St. Paul, © 1984; *Original Unity of Man and Woman: Catechesis on the Book of Genesis.* Boston, MA, Daughters of St. Paul, © 1981; *The Theology of Marriage and Celibacy: Catechesis on Marriage and Celibacy and the Resurrection of the Body.* Boston, MA: Daughters of St. Paul, © 1986.

1993. The encyclical *Veritatis Splendor* was intended to coincide with the publication of the *Catechism of the Catholic Church.* It was not the task of the new catechism to become embroiled in theological debate. Through the new catechism a lucid understanding of the mystery of redemption and an authentic interpretation of the ten commandments is set forth in print.[7] This work will form the foundation for the development of updated catechetical materials that will serve the Catholic Church into the twenty-first century and beyond.

The catechism is divided into the following four parts:

(I) The Profession of Faith
(II) The Celebration of the Christian Mystery
(III) Life in Christ
(IV) Christian Prayer.

It presents an organic and systematic exposition of the essential contents and fundamental Catholic doctrine in the light of Vatican Council II. The catechism's sources are Sacred Scripture, the writings of the Church Fathers (patristics), the liturgy and the Church's Magisterium.[8]

The third part, *Life in Christ,* contains a complete and systematic catechesis where the encyclical limits itself to specific fundamental questions. The first section addresses the dignity of the human person (chapter 1), the human community (chapter 2), the divine gift of salvation (chapter 3). The second section explains the significance of the Decalogue. Chapter 1 makes clear the obligations of the commandments with reference to God; and chapter 2, the obligations regarding our neighbors.

---

7. Joseph Cardinal Ratzinger, "The Catechism of the Catholic Church and the Optimism of the Redeemed," *Communio* 20 (Fall 1993): 501-504.

8. *Catéchism de l'Église catholique*, (Ottawa, Canada: Concacan Inc. pour Liberia Editrice Vaticana, 1993): 13.

To Whom It Is Addressed and the Expectations of Leadership

The encyclical *Veritatis Splendor* is not written for casual reading. It is one of the few papal encyclicals in recent memory that directs its efforts to a specific group. It is addressed...to all the bishops of the Catholic Church regarding "certain fundamental questions of the Church's moral teaching..." (n. 5). It appeals to them as the primary educators of the faithful and encourages them to exercise the responsibility given to them by their ordination. The task of theologians, as they assist the faithful in discerning and understanding the faith, is refined in the light of authentic Church teaching that has been given since the close of Vatican II.

Veritatis Splendor addresses fundamental points about theological method and the validity of specific schools of thought associated with developments that emerged over the past thirty years. The wide range of responses cited in the bibliography (page 59) bears testimony to the impact of the Pope's teaching. Rabbi Jacob Neusner's comment on the encyclical is insightful and reflects many of the current commentators:

> *Amid the glorious plurality of humanity, the Pope insists, here is a single standard of truth and morality. He would have been derelict, had he not made clear what he knows that standard to be.*[9]

In the past, public assent to papal statements among most Catholic theologians was the norm. In the face of the application of modern democratic values and the advancing ideals of cultural pluralism and self-determination, a *hermeneutic of suspicion* emerged as the favored mode of operation for theological investigation. The emphasis upon a more "democratic"

9. Jacob Neusner, "Single Standard of Truth," *Crisis* 11, No. 11, (Wednesday, Dec. 1, 1993): 41-43.

approach to moral matters led to confusion between moral principles, critical opinion and popular consensus. The advances made in public education and literacy, the rapid ascent of social communications through the past century, and the contemporary appetite for succinct resolution of complex issues has led many to embrace a subjective approach to moral decision-making. This has been most evident in North America, where the mass media have exerted an inestimable influence in the formation of modern consciousness.

Lisa Sowle Cahill comments on this situation in the light of *Veritatis Splendor*. She notes:

> *North American culture...exhibits pluralism, values freedom, and often accommodates moral confusion by resorting to guarantees of free choice and informed consent. Not wanting to be dogmatic or totalitarian, we edge away from difficult and divisive decisions about the morally best action or policy. Hence we find it difficult to advance toward substantive public consensus about the human good or the good society.*[10]

The connection between modern culture and the Church's efforts in proclaiming the Gospel has been a mark of the teachings of Pope John Paul II. He states:

> *Since the beginning of my pontificate I have considered the Church's dialogue with the cultures of our time to be a vital area, one in which the destiny of the world, at the end of the twentieth century, is at stake.*[11]

Having reviewed the basis for the development of the encyclical, we now move to the document's actual content.

---

10. Lisa Sowle Cahill, "Veritatis Splendor," *Commonweal*, CXX, No. 18 (Oct. 22, 1993): 15.

11. From a Letter to Agostino Cardinal Cassaroli on the establishment of the Pontifical Council for Culture (1982), cited in A. Dulles, "The Prophetic Humanism of John Paul II," *America* (Oct. 23, 1993): 9.

What Does the Encyclical Look Like?

Introduction

Jesus Christ, the True Light....—nn. 1-3

The Purpose of the Present Encyclical—nn. 4-5

A. Chapter 1: Teacher...What Good Must I Do...

Someone came to him....—nn. 6-7 (Mt 19:16)

Teacher, what good must I do to have eternal life?—n. 8

There is only one who is good—nn. 9-11 (Mt 19:17)

If you wish to enter into life, keep the commandments—nn. 12-15 (Mt 19:17)

If you wish to be perfect—nn. 16-18 (Mt 19:21)

Come, follow me—nn. 19-21 (Mt 19:21)

With God all things are possible—nn. 22-24 (Mt 19:26)

Lo, I am with you always, to the close of the age—nn. 25-27 (Mt 28:20)

B. Chapter 2: Do Not Be Conformed to This World

Teaching what befits sound doctrine—nn. 28-30 (Titus 2:1)

You will know the truth, and the truth will make you free—nn. 31-34

I. Freedom and Law

Of the tree of the knowledge of good and evil you shall not eat—nn. 35-37

God left man in the power of his own counsel—nn. 38-41

Blessed is the man who takes delight in the law of the Lord—nn. 42-45

What the law requires is written on their hearts—nn. 46-50

From the beginning it was not so—nn. 51-53

II. Conscience and Truth

Man's sanctuary—nn. 54-56

The judgment of conscience—nn. 57-61

Seeking what is true and good—nn. 62-64

III. Fundamental Choice and Specific Kinds of Behavior

Only do not use your freedom as an opportunity for the flesh—nn. 65-68

Mortal and venial sin—nn. 69-70

IV. The Moral Act

Teleology and teleologism—nn. 71-75

The object of the deliberate act—nn. 76-78

"Intrinsic evil": it is not licit to do evil that good may come of it—nn. 79-83

C. Chapter 3: Lest the Cross of Christ Be Emptied of Its Power

For freedom Christ has set us free—nn. 84-87

Walking in the light—nn. 88-89

Martyrdom, the exaltation of the inviolable holiness of God's law—nn. 90-94

Universal and unchanging moral norms at the service of the person and of society—nn. 95-97

Morality and the renewal of social and political life—nn. 98-101

Grace and obedience to God's law—nn. 102-105

Morality and the new evangelization—nn. 106-108

The service of moral theologians—nn. 109-113

Our own responsibilities as pastors—nn. 114-117

D. Conclusion

Mary, Mother of Mercy—nn. 118-120

Within the encyclical, key themes are developed. They include the following:

The relationship of natural law to truth
The objectivity of truth and the role of conscience
The objectivity of divine law
The relationship between law and freedom
The testimony of Scripture

—The subordination of man and human activity to God
—The relationship between the moral good of human acts and eternal life
—The nature of Christian discipleship
—The gift of the Holy Spirit

The mandate of the Church to teach the truth
—The guidance of the Holy Spirit

The stance of the human person before the truth
—human moral action

The role of witness in the proclamation of the Gospel
—Christians are called to bear a living testimony by the life of the Holy Spirit given in Baptism.
—Christian witness includes a radical stance against moral evil and sin

What to Look For, What to Overlook, and What **Not** *to Look For at All*

Veritatis Splendor sets out to correct some serious moral errors. It reaffirms the fundamental Tradition of the Church and its use of natural moral law. The encyclical also presents a heightened appreciation of the nature and role of Sacred Scripture against tortured ethical systems of the present and the past. The encyclical makes clear the fundamental aspects of Catholic moral doctrine in the face of certain controversial problems of present-day moral theology. It is addressed to all the bishops of the Catholic Church, who share with the Pope the responsibility of preserving "sound teaching." In that light, *Veritatis Splendor* is a technical document, carefully and painstakingly advancing those propositions that accurately reflect the Church's Tradition.

The encyclical points out, and even stands as an example of how moral reflection continues to develop as the Christian community is challenged by new situations. A general and systematic calling into question of traditional moral doctrine seem to have become popular in recent years. Such a challenge was founded upon anthropological and ethical concepts that separate mankind from the Creator. The corrective "lens" of consistent Church teaching presented in this document clarifies the points of doctrine needed in resolving this crisis of faith (*VS* nn. 10, 12, 110-111).

Legitimate theological inquiry is clearly promoted by the Holy Father, but *Veritatis* seeks to restore the rightful balance in theological analysis. This occurs only when human reason is enriched by God's own grace. Theological reflection originates as a service to the Church and must remain so. Theologians are called first and foremost to be faithful to Christ and his Church (n. 109 ff.).

There are no condemnations of individuals here. Nobody is judging anybody else. No villains are named, nor people denounced. The clear call of the Pope in this encyclical is to conversion of the whole self to Jesus Christ. There is no disapproval of the social and empirical sciences. On the contrary their contributions are praised. It is the over-extension of these fields, across the horizon of revealed truth, that the faithful are cautioned against.

Pastoral Applications

Veritatis Splendor provides the official challenging response to the secular world's vision of truth. One critique of modern theological methodology advances the need to include discipleship more clearly in the examination of doctrines. The personal acceptance of Christ as Savior lies at the heart of Catholic moral theology and pastoral care. Assent to Christ and Christ's authority *through* the Magisterium is a critical point raised by the encyclical. Put clearly, the rejection of the Magisterium is a rejection of Christ's headship.

A theology that is constructed apart from acknowledging the authority of Christ is inadequate to assist the personal maturation of the Christian community. Over the years a substantial thrust for solid academic and spiritual formation for pastoral care workers, clergy and laity alike, has been nurtured by the Church. The encyclical *Veritatis Splendor* clearly presents the task of discipleship as inseparable from moral thought and behavior. A careful reading of the document and its commentaries will assist in providing a balanced vision of Christian moral thought and moral behavior.

Graduate and Seminary Formation

The encyclical spells out the normative force of the Church's moral teaching. This booklet outlines the encyclical to make reading the full text less difficult. Nothing substitutes for reading the primary document. *Veritatis Splendor* is addressed to a specific group (the bishops of the Catholic Church). The approach and language conform to a formal presentation of the foundations of moral theology. This booklet serves as a "gateway" for understanding the encyclical and the issues that surround it.

A glossary defining terms is found within this work. The commentary gives a brief view of the background that shaped the writing of the encyclical and should ground the reader in his or her appreciation of *Veritatis Splendor.* The section on "Current Controversies" provides the reader with a comparison of contrasting moral methods.

Formal Education Programs

The impact of Pope John Paul II has been remarkable. Each of his encyclicals has received widespread commentary in the popular press. These encyclicals have appeared on the front page of the *New York Times*, highlighting the force of

Catholic moral teaching in society. The moral ambiguity of contemporary American thinking, and this applies beyond the geopolitical confines of the United States, and mass media's "soup of-the-day" approach to ethical issues require a clear, courageous and consistent witness to the Truth.

The general level of education of the laity has risen sharply since Pope Leo XIII first began using encyclicals as an important tool for teaching. The level of faith has often not matched the educational advances, particularly in the present day and especially in the "post-Christian" west. The language of any encyclical is first and foremost one of faith. Outside of faith in Christ, papal encyclicals are significant only as one ethical vision among many. Read within the horizon of revealed truth, papal encyclicals can be seen as a sign of the guidance of the Holy Spirit and apt tools for forming the faithful's conscience.

Touching the Truth provides a vehicle from which an interested and educated laity can come to a fuller appreciation of the vitality of the Catholic tradition in the modern world. The materials provided within the booklet can expand a reader's viewpoint. They also provide the ground from which a fruitful discussion of Catholic moral teaching can take place.

Summary Outline

Veritatis Splendor: the Splendor of Truth

Pope John Paul II

August 6, 1993

Introduction

Jesus Christ, the True Light.... (nn. 1-3)

The human response to the truth is weakened through sin. Nonetheless, the human search for truth continues in all fields of human endeavor (n. 1).

Only through Jesus Christ and through his Church is an adequate response to fundamental questions about the meaning of life offered (n. 2).

As morality touches each human, the way of salvation opens to all. The Church is the authoritative guide on this path (n. 3).

The Purpose of the Present Encyclical (nn. 4-5)

The different spheres of human life have brought forth troubling issues:

—the rejection of consistent moral teaching

—the exaltation of dissent grounded in social sciences

—the rejection of the link between faith and moral life (n. 4).

The specific purpose of the encyclical is twofold:

—to respond to the question of dissent

—to provide principles of moral judgment grounded in Scripture and Tradition (n. 5).

A. Teacher...What Good Must I Do...?

Someone came to him.... (nn. 6-7)

Mt 19:16 "Then someone came to him...."

Matthew's account of the rich young man illustrates those who approach Christ with questions about the full meaning of human life. The task of the Church is to lead others to Christ (nn. 6-7).

Teacher, what good must I do to have eternal life? (n. 8)

The question asked by the rich young man and Jesus' reply are the basis for understanding the heart of Gospel-centered moral teaching (n. 8).

There is only one who is good (nn. 9-11)

Mt 19:17 And he said to him, "Why do you ask me about what is good? There is only one who is good."

To ask about the Good means to turn toward God, the source of human fulfillment (n. 9).

Authentic moral life is the fitting response of men and women made in the image of their Creator (n. 10). As God alone is the source of good, human goodness comes as solely a gift from God (n. 11).

If you wish to enter into life, keep the commandments (nn. 12-15).

Mt 19:17 "If you wish to enter into life, keep the commandments."

God alone is the Good. Human nature, created by God, was disfigured by sin. Through the commandments revealed at Sinai, God has unveiled what is good to humanity. Following the commandments is linked to the promise of the Kingdom of God, definitively revealed in Jesus (n. 12).

The Ten Commandments are the basis of Christian moral life and present the basic condition for living it. They protect the singular dignity of the human person and advance each person's good (n. 13).

There is an inseparable unity between the two great commandments, attested to by the words, life and mission of Christ (n. 14).

Jesus shows that the commandments are the foundation of human life and the starting point on the path to perfection. In the "Sermon on the Mount" Jesus brings God's commandments to fulfillment. It is Jesus who is both the fulfillment and source of this law (n. 15).

If you wish to be perfect (nn. 16-18)

Mt 19:21 Jesus said to him, "If you wish to be perfect, go, sell your possessions and give the money to the poor, and you will have treasure in heaven…."

Jesus, the fulfillment of the Law, reveals in the beatitudes the basis of discipleship. Authentic Christian moral life goes beyond the legalistic vision of the commandments. Jesus himself is the vision of true discipleship and calls all to follow (n. 16).

Growth toward perfection requires maturity in self-giving and God's gift of grace. One must acknowledge the power of sin and the presence of human weakness (n. 17).

The call to follow Jesus arises from the Holy Spirit and draws one beyond legal demands. The invitation given to the young man brings forth the full meaning of the commandments to love one's neighbor and to love God (n. 18).

Come, follow me (nn. 19-21)

Mt 19:21 "…then come, follow me."

The call to discipleship is initiated by Christ himself. Following Christ is the foundation of Christian morality. The person of Jesus presents the radical call to discipleship in every generation (n. 19).

To love *as* Jesus loves, fully, completely and without reservation, constitutes the moral rule of Christian life (n. 20).

With God all things are possible (nn. 22-24)

Mt 19:26 But Jesus looked at them and said, "With men it is impossible, but with God all things are possible."

Following Christ means becoming conformed to him in the depth of the human heart. This is an effect of grace, the presence of the Holy Spirit in the believer. By the work of the Holy Spirit, one becomes a member of his Body, the Church, whose unity in Christ culminates in sharing the Eucharist (n. 21).

The demands of Christ are impossible through human effort alone. The power to imitate Christ and to live out that love comes only through the gift of that love from the Father through the Son, which is the Spirit (n. 22).

The Law reveals human powerlessness and the necessity of divine grace in living the Christian life (n. 23).

The possibility of authentic love comes exclusively through the grace of the Holy Spirit given as a gift. The knowledge of this gift of grace generates and sustains the free response of the disciple. "The New Law is the grace of the Holy Spirit given through faith in Christ" (n. 24).

Lo, I am with you always, to the close of the age (nn. 25-27)

Mt 28:20 "...and teaching them to obey everything that I have commanded you. And remember, I am with you always, to the end of the age."

The moral teaching revealed by Christ must be both faithfully kept and practiced under the guidance of the Holy Spirit in all cultures and throughout history (n. 25).

From the beginning of the Church, no separation between faith and life was admitted. Constant pastoral vigilance to the integrity of faith and life has always been for the protection of the unity of the Church (n. 26).

The living Tradition that comes from the apostles to our own age progresses under the guidance of the Holy Spirit. The authentic interpretation of that living Tradition has been entrusted to the Church's Magisterium (n. 27).

B. Do Not Be Conformed to This World

Teaching what befits sound doctrine (nn. 28-30)

Titus 2:1 "But as for you, teach what is consistent with sound doctrine."

Throughout both Testaments the essential elements of revelation about moral action are detailed:

—The subordination of humans and their activity to God

—The relationship between the moral good of human acts and eternal life

—Christian discipleship as revealing the nature of perfect love

—The Gift of the Holy Spirit, the source and means of authentic moral life.

The Church, moved by the Spirit, has faithfully preserved what the word of God proclaims about truths and also moral action. The Church has achieved a doctrinal development regarding moral action analogous to that of dogma (n. 28).

The nature of moral theology is described:

—Moral theology examines the good and evil of human acts and of the person who performs them, recognizing that the origin and end of moral action are found in God and offered through Christ.

—Theologians must find suitable ways, based in Sacred Scripture, to communicate moral teaching to the people of their particular place and age.

—This work of theologians has already born fruit through reflections better formed to address the issues of the present age.

—The context of debate following the Council produced certain interpretations inconsistent with "sound teaching." Though no one theological or philosophical system can be imposed, certain trends clearly are incompatible (n. 29).

This encyclical presents the bishops with fundamental principles to discern what is contrary to sound doctrine. The

Church carries out the task of dogmatic and moral reflection within an interdisciplinary context, necessary in facing new issues (n. 30).

You will know the truth, and the truth will make you free (nn. 31-34)

Human freedom is the central issue of the age. Respect for the dignity of the human person and conscience is affirmed (n. 31).

The exaggerated exaltation of freedom leads to the distortion of the idea of conscience and is rejected for that reason. The function of the conscience is to apply the universal knowledge of the good in a specific situation and to express a judgment on right conduct (n. 32).

Behavioral sciences explore the very idea of freedom, paradoxically providing important insights yet questioning its very existence, thus denying or at least relativizing morality (n. 33).

The issue of freedom is critical in every moral discussion. There can be no morality without freedom, which comes from and leads to God. Freedom is dependent upon truth (n. 34).

I. Freedom and Law

Of the tree of the knowledge of good and evil you shall not eat (nn. 35-37)

Determining what is good and what is evil belongs not to humanity but to God.

Human freedom finds its fulfillment in accepting the moral law given by God.

God's law protects rather than lessens human freedom.

The conflict between rationalism, relativism and divine law is artificial and ruled out as the ground for moral autonomy (n. 35).

The influence of rationalism and relativism upon the sphere of Catholic moral theology contradicts both Sacred Scripture and the Church's constant teaching.

Human beings, through reason, participate in the moral law, but do not establish it (n. 36).

Some theologians have separated real human activity in this world from that of salvation. Divine revelation itself reveals moral norms and is not merely exhortatory (n. 37).

God left man in the power of his own counsel (nn. 38-41)

Genuine freedom allows us to seek God of our own accord and to share in God's dominion, uncovering in creation the laws placed there by God (n. 38).

In exercising dominion over the world, humanity builds up that perfection intended by God, shaping the world in accord with its own intelligence and will.

Morally good acts bring one to a fuller likeness to God (n. 39).

The role of human reason in moral life draws one into authentic autonomy and is indivisible from the truth and authority of the eternal law. The power of reason cannot mean that reason itself creates values and moral norms (n. 40).

Genuine moral autonomy means the acceptance of the moral law.

The allegation of heteronomy (an absolute rule from the outside) in morality sharply contradicts both revelation and the incarnation. This runs contrary to the dignity of the human person.

The possibility of obedience implies that human reason and will participate in the wisdom of God, expressed especially in divine law (n. 41).

Blessed is the man who takes delight in the law of the Lord (nn. 42-45)

Human freedom, patterned on God's own, allows man, through the use of natural reason, to discern good from evil, the function of natural law.

Natural law receives its name because the reason which makes it known is proper to human nature (n. 42).

Man, through the guidance of God, is increasingly able to recognize the eternal truth.

The love and care of God comes from within, that is, through reason, and shows the right direction for humans to take in free actions.

Natural law enters as the human expression of God's eternal law (n. 43).

Human reason, able to distinguish good from evil, is enlightened by divine revelation and by faith. It is called to accept and live out God's law as a sign of election and blessing (n. 44).

The Church both accepts and devoutly preserves the entire deposit of revelation.

Distinctions between revealed and natural law refer always to the same author, who is God.

Both "laws" have their origin in God, support each other and pose no threat to human freedom (n. 45).

What the law requires is written on their hearts (nn. 46-50)

The historical tension between freedom and nature has entered the contemporary arena from the view of scientific methodology and subjectivism.

Considering *nature*, moral facts are equated with statistically verifiable data, with the result that moral behavior and the behavior of the majority are confused.

Freedom is often seen as conflicting with *nature*. It is reduced to biological or social "raw" material for human activity. In this view man is nothing more than his own life project—his personal freedom (n. 46).

From this perspective the primary objection is that *natural law* presents biology as morality, especially in the area of sexuality and conjugal life.

Theologians who hold this objection maintain the claim

that one can and must freely determine the meaning of personal behavior.

In this approach, the love of neighbor becomes an exclusive respect for the freedom to choose. "Natural inclinations" establish only a general orientation and cannot determine the morality of human acts of themselves (n. 47).

Refuting this claim, the Church teaches the unity of the human person "...whose rational soul is *per se et essentialiter* the form of his body" (n. 48).

The person—body and soul—is the subject of his own moral acts and so embraces both a unique spiritual and bodily structure.

The total person therefore is to be loved and respected as an end, never as a means; this suggests the basic goods as those ends to which we are drawn (n. 48).

Teachings that separate moral activity from the bodily exercise of that activity contradict both Scripture and Tradition.

In man there is no separation between person and act; body and soul stand or fall together (n. 49).

Natural law refers to the fundamental nature of the human person in the unity of spiritual and biological inclinations as well as those other elements necessary for the pursuit of his end.

A division between freedom and nature is never possible because of the unified totality of body and soul (n. 50).

From the beginning it was not so (nn. 51-53)

Because it is inscribed in the rational nature of the human person, natural law is universal and immutable. It lays the foundation for the fundamental rights and duties of the human person—embracing each one's free acts (n. 51).

Both positive and negative precepts of the natural law are universally valid.

Positive precepts are those that order us to perform certain actions and cultivate particular dispositions, and are known through practical reason.

Negative precepts forbid specific acts because the choice of this kind of behavior is incompatible with the goodness of the will of the acting person and that person's vocation.

One can be prevented from doing certain good acts but can never be hindered from refraining from bad ones (n. 52).

Questions have been raised about the validity of moral law in the face of culture and history.

While a person exists in a specific culture, that same person is not fully defined through it.

Seeking the most adequate formulation of moral norms in the light of differing cultures is the task of the Church in each generation (n. 53).

II. Conscience and Truth

Man's sanctuary (nn. 54-56)

The relationship between human freedom and divine law presents itself within the moral conscience.

Where freedom is given exaggerated importance and set in opposition to law, tendencies emerge that lead a moral conscience to depart from Church Tradition and the Magisterium (n. 54).

The function of conscience has been diminished to applying general moral norms to individual cases. Conscience leads to a creative and responsible acceptance of those personal tasks entrusted by God; not a detailed observance of universal law. Specific authors fail to call the acts of conscience "judgments," preferring the term "decisions." They claim that only "autonomous" decision-making fosters authentic maturity and that the Church's interventions cause unnecessary conflicts (n. 55).

Justifying this position, authors have promoted a two-level view of moral truth—"doctrinal" and "pastoral." This effectively permits one to do in practice what is intrinsically evil. This separation leads to so-called "pastoral" solutions that run contrary to the Magisterium, challenging the heart of moral conscience (n. 56).

The judgment of conscience (nn. 57-61)

The Letter to the Romans provides the biblical understanding of conscience and its connection to law. Conscience makes its witness only to the person and in turn only that person knows their own response to it (n. 57).

This inner dialogue is also a dialogue with God, commanding with a binding force. Through the conscience one is made open to the voice of God (n. 58).

Conscience is a practical moral judgment about a person and his action, making clear the moral obligation—what one must or must not do, or what has already been done. Conscience applies the law to the specific case, an application that becomes an inner dictate to do what is good in the particular "here and now" (n. 59).

One must act in accord with one's conscience. Acting contrary, or when in doubt, one stands condemned by one's conscience, the proximate norm of personal morality. The judgment of conscience bears witness to the natural law (n. 60).

The judgment of conscience recognizes the truth about moral good. The verdict of conscience bears witness to the good as well as to the malice of a particular choice. It also remains as a pledge of divine mercy, calling one beyond the evil done to ask reconciliation with God.

The authentic link between freedom and truth is made clear in the practical judgment of conscience (n. 61).

Seeking what is true and good (nn. 62-64)

Conscience is not infallible and can err in its judgment. This can be the result of *invincible ignorance* as well as other factors (n. 62).

The dignity of the conscience derives from the truth.

The correct conscience receives the objective truth correctly.

The erroneous conscience confuses the subjective view with objective truth.

The conscience is culpable and in error when one fails to seek the truth (cf. Mt 6:22-23) (n. 63).

The call to form one's conscience comes from Christ himself. Through the Church and her Magisterium, authentic truth is taught with the authority that comes from Christ.

The Church serves the conscience, assisting it to attain the truth with surety (n. 64).

III. Fundamental Choice and Specific Kinds of Behavior

Only do not use your freedom as an opportunity for the flesh (nn. 65-68)

The concept of "fundamental option" diminishes particular acts and is rejected. In this framework human acts are seen as partial steps in self-determination.

Human activity becomes disjointed when the will is separated from concrete behaviors. Moral good gets determined by the fundamental option, separated from concrete behavior (n. 65).

Biblical foundations for a fundamental and free commitment to God are clear (n. 66).

One's particular choices of specific actions affirm one's fundamental choice and are inseparable from it. One cannot determine the morality of specific human acts from a non-specific orientation disconnected from one's actual moral life (n. 67).

Condemnation does not come to a person only through some infidelity to a fundamental option for God. Every mortal sin offends God as the giver of law; even if one perseveres in faith, the loss of "sanctifying grace" is the critical point (n. 68).

Mortal and venial sin (nn. 69-70)

The gravity of sin, within the understanding of a fundamental option, centers on the degree of freedom of the acting person rather than the matter of the act. The traditional distinctions between mortal and venial sin are thus blurred (n. 69).

The importance and validity of the distinction between mortal and venial sin is affirmed. Man's fundamental orientation can be radically changed by specific acts. A rejection of this is a denial of Catholic doctrine (n. 70).

IV. The Moral Act

Teleology and teleologism (nn. 71-75)

Through human acts one comes to perfection. Human acts are moral acts because they express and determine the moral disposition of the one performing those acts. Within their deliberateness, they give moral definition to the person who carries out these acts (n. 71).

Human acts are morally good when they attest to and express the voluntary ordering of the person and the conformity of a concrete action to that ultimate end confirmed by reason (n. 72).

There is a teleological character to moral life because God is the supreme good and the ultimate end (telos) of man. This aspect of the human person is objective because human acts are capable of being ordered to this end (n. 73).

The traditional "sources of morality"—the intention of the actor, the circumstances and especially the consequences of the act, as well as the object of the act—are identified. Distinctions made in "teleological" ethical theories between non-moral or pre-moral values are spelled out. The legitimacy of such investigation is explained (n. 74).

Two primary theories have emerged in contemporary moral thought—*consequentialism* and *proportionalism.*

Consequentialism proposes that the criteria of right action derive solely from the calculation of foreseeable consequences drawn from a specific choice.

Proportionalism focuses upon weighing the good against the bad effects of a particular choice.

Both theories acknowledge the following:

1. moral values are indicated by reason and revelation

2. moral values can never be formulated into absolute and specific prohibitions across history or culture.

Moral responsibility appears in two ways:

1. moral goods (e.g. love of God, of neighbor, justice)

2. pre-moral goods (also called "non-moral, physical or ontic...for example...loss of material goods, life, death").

Moral acts are judged from two bases:

1. moral "goodness" that derives from the person's intentions in reference to moral goods

2. moral "rightness" that reflects the consideration of foreseeable consequences and the proportion between

a. the act and its effects

b. the effects themselves and regard the pre-moral order alone.

Moral "goodness" is determined exclusively by fidelity to the highest values, independent of particular moral precepts.

These precepts remain operative, but as relative norms (n. 75).

The object of the deliberate act (nn. 76-78)

The persuasive force of these arguments lies in their focus upon measurement and does not reflect authentic Church teaching based on divine and natural law.

Specific moral precepts, presented by the Church, are binding upon the faithful (n. 76).

Weighing these foreseeable consequences is inadequate for moral evaluations.

Though capable of affecting the moral gravity of an act, these foreseeable consequences cannot alter the moral identity of that act.

Evaluating and calculating all the consequences is impossible (n. 77).

The morality of a human act depends on the rationally chosen "object," freely and willfully chosen by the acting person.

Specific types of behavior emerge from a disordered will, that is to say, a will ordered toward evil rather than good.

Human acts are perfected when the will is directed, through charity, to God (n. 78).

"Intrinsic evil": it is not licit to do evil that good may come of it (nn. 79-83)

Proportionalist and consequentialist teleological principles must be rejected because the decisive and basic element for moral judgment is the object of the human act.

This object establishes the capacity of an act's being ordered toward or away from God.

Only an orientation to God perfects the human person.

Knowledge of this order is found within human nature and is safeguarded by the commandments (n. 79).

Reason makes evident that certain human acts radically contradict the good of the person. These are "intrinsically evil" acts. Euthanasia, voluntary suicide, and contraception are examples of these acts (n. 80).

The evil in acts can be diminished by a good intention or specific circumstances, yet it cannot be removed (n. 81).

The doctrine of the object as the source of morality is solidly biblical.

The moral quality of human activity is yoked to fidelity to the commandments.

The rejection of proportionalist and consequentialist views is restated; the claim for exceptionless norms is advanced. Good intentions are qualified as those that have the true good of the person in view of his ultimate end (n. 82).

The teaching of the Church is grounded in the truth about human nature. Bishops are exhorted not merely to warn about error but to show the faithful the person and power of Jesus Christ (n. 83).

C. Lest the Cross of Christ Be Emptied of Its Power

For freedom Christ has set us free (nn. 84-87)

The relationship between human freedom and truth is seen as the fundamental question in moral theology. The Church, against the challenge of relativism, needs to develop a pastoral response regarding this precise point (n. 84).

In her constant looking to the crucified Lord, the Church discerns the fullest revelation of the meaning of freedom and finds the foundation of its power to teach (n. 85).

Human freedom, real yet limited, is an essential part of our creaturely nature, is the basis for the dignity of the person, and is directed toward communion with God (n. 86).

Knowledge of the crucified and risen Lord Jesus is the timeless source from which the Church sets forth its vision of the human person and authentic freedom (n. 87).

Walking in the light (nn. 88-89)

One of the most distressing results of believers' placing truth against freedom is the separation of morality from faith. Authentic Christian faith is a lived knowledge of Jesus Christ and his teachings, not simply intellectual assent to specific propositions (n. 88).

Authentic moral life is both a confession and a witness. Christ's witness is the source, model and means for the believer (n. 89).

Martyrdom, the exaltation of the inviolable holiness of God's law (nn. 90-94)

Certain teleological approaches, e.g. consequentialism and proportionalism, reject the existence of negative moral norms. They are unacceptable, since moral norms protect the personal dignity of every human being (n. 90).

The examples of Susanna, John the Baptist, Stephen, James and other martyrs are offered by the Church as models in the defense of moral truth even unto death (n. 91).

Martyrdom affirms the inviolability of the moral order and is an outstanding sign of the holiness of the Church (n. 92).

The Christian is called, with the grace of God, and taking sometimes heroic measures, to stand as a witness to the truth of the moral order (n. 93).

The Christian does not stand alone as a witness to the fact that there exist inviolable truths and moral values for which one must be prepared to sacrifice even one's life (n. 94).

Universal and unchanging moral norms at the service of the person and of society (nn. 95-97)

The firmness of the Church's teaching about universal moral norms does not diminish her maternal love and compassion for all (n. 95).

The Church's firmness about this matter is offered as a service to every human person as the foundation for human equality (n. 96).

Negative moral norms are those that prohibit evil, protect human dignity, preserve society and its rightful development. No one has the authority to violate the fundamental and inalienable rights of the human person (n. 97).

Morality and the renewal of social and political life (nn. 98-101)

Outrage over violated human rights sends forth the call for a radical transformation of particular "cultural" views (n. 98).

Transcendent truth makes it impossible to construct a totalitarian social order, one that denies the dignity of the human person (n. 99).

Specific offenses against the human person, listed within the *Catechism of the Catholic Church*, are delineated. The practice of the virtues of temperance and justice and of solidarity are specified (n. 100).

Ethical relativism remains a threat to the dignity of the human person and the moral vision of political and social life.

The critical role of objective moral norms is reaffirmed in all political structures (n. 101).

Grace and obedience to God's law (nn. 102-105)

The inner division experienced within human life concerning good and evil can be overcome only by the grace of God (n. 102).

Believers always find the grace and strength to keep God's law in the saving cross of Christ the Redeemer, in the gift of the Holy Spirit and the sacraments (n. 103).

Human frailty, even in the light of God's mercy, is never the basis from which to judge human acts (n. 104).

A false and pharasaical piety, which weighs what one "can do" against what one "must do" violates authentic devotion (n. 105).

Morality and the new evangelization (nn. 106-108)

The powerful challenge of evangelization originates as a mandate of the risen Christ. The decay of Christian life and values arises from cultural and moral relativism as well as the loss of appreciation for the Gospel (n. 106).

Intrinsic to a renewed evangelization is the proclamation and presentation of moral truth. The Christian life of holiness brings to completion the prophetic, priestly and royal work which is given in Baptism. The saints, particularly the Virgin Mother of God, are the exemplars of this work (n. 107).

The very *Spirit of Christ* is the principle and strength of the Church and its mandate for morality and evangelization (n. 108).

The service of moral theologians (nn. 109-113)

As theology is a service to the Church, the vocation of the theologian in the Church is to pursue "an ever deeper understanding of the word of God found in the inspired Scriptures and handed on by the living Tradition of the Church…in communion with the Magisterium..." (n. 109).

Because the spheres of faith and moral life are inseparable, the Magisterium has the task of *discerning* the truths about faith and morality. All theologians are called to give loyal assent, as part of their ministry, to the Magisterium's teachings in faith and moral life (n. 110).

Moral theologians serve both the Church and the broader human society in the search for authentic moral life. The normative dimension of moral teachings can never be reduced to behavioral or natural science (n. 111).

Though beneficial, behavioral sciences need to be used prudently by the moral theologian. "The affirmation of moral principles is not within the competence of formal empirical methods." The starting point for moral theology must be faithful to the spiritual dimension of the human heart and its vocation to divine love (n. 112).

Moral theologians are called to train the faithful in moral judgment. Moral teaching goes beyond the capacity of democratic processes. Orchestrated dissent, clear opposition, is not a legitimate expression either of Christian freedom or of the diversity of the gifts of the Spirit. Christian pastors have the duty to insure that the faithful receive authentic Catholic teaching in its entirety (n. 113).

Our own responsibilities as Pastors (nn. 114-117)

The bishops have the common duty and grace to teach the faithful according to the model of Jesus. The prophetic, priestly and royal service is central to pastoral duty (n. 114).

This encyclical marks the first time the Magisterium has detailed these pastoral principles. It reaffirms "the universality and immutability of the moral commandments," in particular those concerning "intrinsically evil acts" (n. 115).

Under the guidance of the Holy Spirit and in communion with the Apostolic See, it is the duty of bishops to be vigilant in these matters, especially in the overseeing of *Catholic institutions* (n. 116).

The voice of the Church in moral matters echoes that of Christ. The anointing of the Holy Spirit, given to every Christian, allows the "gentle but challenging word" to become "light and life" for everyone (n. 117).

Conclusion

Mary, Mother of Mercy (nn. 118-120)

The title of Mary as Mother of Mercy is grounded in her mission as the Mother of Christ—the incarnation of God's mercy. This divine mercy reaches its fullness in the gift of the Holy Spirit (n. 118).

Though Christian morality can appear complex, Christian morality is in fact living the life of Christ, abandoning oneself to him and allowing oneself to be transformed by his grace. The task of the teaching authority of the Church is to oversee this dynamic process of following Christ free from falsehood and error (n. 119).

Mary is the Mother of Mercy, as Jesus entrusts his Church and all humanity to her. She is the model of the moral life in her self-donation and free acceptance of God's will. Sharing our human condition, yet free from sin, Mary recalls the authentic demands of morality to all ages and places, and that only Christ himself fulfills the human hope (n. 120).

Key Quotes from the Encyclical

These citations summarize many of the main points of this encyclical. They can serve as starting points for personal reflection and even as a basis for specific presentations, lectures and sermons.

"The moral life presents itself as the response due to the many gratuitous initiatives taken by God out of love for man. It is a response of love..." (n. 10).

"From the very lips of Jesus, the new Moses, man is once again given the commandments of the Decalogue. Jesus himself definitively confirms them and proposes them to us as the way and condition of salvation" (n. 12).

"God's law does not reduce, much less do away with human freedom; rather, it protects and promotes that freedom" (n. 35).

"Patterned on God's freedom, man's freedom is not negated by his obedience to the divine law; indeed, only through this obedience does it abide in the truth and conform to human dignity" (n. 42).

"In his journey toward God, the One who 'alone is good,' man must freely do good and avoid evil. But in order to accomplish this he must *be able to distinguish good from evil*" (n. 42).

"Conscience [is] the proximate norm of personal morality.... 'Divine law' [is] the universal and objective norm of morality. The judgment of conscience does not establish the law; rather it bears witness to the authority of the natural law..." (n. 60).

"Mortal sin exists when a person knowingly and willingly, for whatever reason, chooses something gravely disordered" (n. 70).

"Human acts are moral acts because they express and determine the goodness or evil of the individual who performs them" (n. 71).

"Pope Paul VI teaches: '...It is never lawful, even for the gravest reasons, to do evil that good may come of it.... If acts are intrinsically evil, a good intention or particular circumstances can diminish their evil, but they cannot remove it'" (nn. 80, 81).

"The voice of conscience has always clearly recalled that there are truths and moral values for which one must be prepared to give up one's life" (n. 94).

"The Church's firmness in defending the universal and unchanging moral norms is not demeaning at all. Its only purpose is to serve man's true freedom" (n. 96).

"What is unacceptable is the attitude of one who makes his own weakness the criterion of the truth about the good, so that he can feel self-justified..." (n. 104).

"Opposition to the teaching of the Church's pastors cannot be seen as a legitimate expression either of Christian freedom or of the diversity of the Spirit's gifts" (n. 113).

"No absolution offered by beguiling doctrines, even in the areas of philosophy and theology, can make man truly happy: only the cross and the glory of the Risen Christ can grant peace to his conscience and salvation to his life" (n. 120).

Glossary

Knowing some implications of these terms is important for having a good knowledge of moral theology. These terms are used continuously in discussions about moral theology. We present them here so you can understand how the encyclical applies these terms. Sources cited in the additional bibliography may help you to further understand these terms.

Anthropology: Theological anthropology. In this sector of theology humans are considered not alone but in relation to God for human origin, nature, condition, dignity and destiny. Through "original sin" man is estranged from God and the human image of God is marred. With the Incarnation of Christ, the marred image is re-created.

Conscience: Designates our awareness of moral truth. A properly formed conscience does not refer to one's feelings of approval or disapproval but to a reflective moral judgment. An informed Catholic conscience will be inclined to embrace as true the authoritative teachings of the Church through which Christ speaks.

Encyclical: The contents of an encyclical belong to the ordinary Magisterium, teachings that have been accepted and taught by the Church throughout the ages. While the encyclical is not infallible, Catholics are nevertheless obliged to accept its doctrinal and moral content (cf. *Catholic Encyclopedia*).

Fundamental Option: Most of these theories shift the focus of self-determination from the free choices we make every day to an alleged act of total self-disposition deep within the person that remains pre-reflexive and incapable of being articulated explicitly in one's consciousness. These theories for the most part fail to take free choice seriously; thus, according to them, some sorts of acts (e.g. adultery), traditionally considered to be mortal sins, even if done deliberately and after sufficient reflection, are not mortal sins but only "grave" ones.

Hermeneutic of Suspicion: *Hermeneutics* refers to principles, methods and rules for the interpretation of literary texts. Interpretation refers to a twofold process that begins with uncovering the meaning of the original text (exegesis) and ends with determining the meaning of that same text for the current reader (cf. *Dictionary of Pentecostal and Charismatic Movements*). The hermeneutic of suspicion begins by questioning the basis for the normative or traditional reading of a passage and seeks to posit alternative grounds for interpreting passages.

Magisterium: According to Vatican II, every bishop by ordination receives a share in the ecclesiastical teaching power. A necessary condition for exercising this role is that the bishop be in hierarchical communion with the episcopal college, in which the Pope is recognized as having a pre-eminent Magisterium in view of his role as the successor of Peter. As pastors, the bishops have the responsibility to see that teaching is done (cf. *Lumen Gentium 21*).

Moral Absolutes: These are negative precepts (You shall not. . .) that show us what love cannot mean. They tell us that some human choices (e.g. abortion), integral actions in themselves, damage and destroy what is good in ourselves and others—even if done for the noblest motives.

Mortal Sin: It is a sin that involves grave matter, i.e. matter judged by the Church to be incompatible with the life to which one is called. It requires sufficient reflection and an adequately free human choice. Even non-believers recognize that morally evil choices involving matter of this kind are utterly incompatible with a commitment to lead morally upright lives, for non-believers too have in their hearts the natural law, their own way of participating in God's loving plan for human existence.

Natural Law: Self-evident principles. "Natural law is nothing other than the participation of eternal law in rational creatures"—St. Thomas Aquinas. The imprint of God's providential plan on man's natural reason. Relation to external law and positive law: the eternal law is its hidden root; the natural law is the main trunk; the different systems of positive law are its branches.

Relativism: In the area of religious thought relativism is based on the assumption that the variables in human thought processes substantially affect one's faith. Moral relativism holds that the moral code of Christianity will vary in relation to the circumstances of the age, the degree of penetration achieved by human persons into the religious psyche or the stage of progress the human race has reached.

Teleology: A term used for a doctrine of final causality (goal, end, completion). Teleology is something experimentally observable: by observing effects it is possible to determine the nature of the agent. Thus, scientific objectivity precludes any value judgments as to what is good or bad in the natural world. The teleological explanation does not rest on any assumption about the cosmos, the human person and his dependency on God.

Theological Dissent: There is no pre or post Vatican II document that supports theological dissent. A theologian who alleges this right to dissent from the authoritative teachings of the Magisterium acts wrongly and does a great disservice to the Church (cf. May, *An Introduction to Moral Theology*, p. 216).

Totalitarianism: A power system directed by a group that pretends to answer all questions and to solve all problems by its doctrine, while it adapts itself to all situations according to the decisions and interests of the ruling elite. Their leaders take the place of God and their ideologies replace and supersede religion.

Venial Sin: This sin, while immoral and incompatible with perfect love, is pardonable since it would not be completely incompatible with a commitment to Christian moral living.

Questions

Three levels of questions are offered here. The *basic* questions are discussion starters for anyone who wants to enrich his or her understanding of the Catholic faith. The *advanced* questions are directed to those who seek a deeper inquiry. The *academic* questions are intended for those whose interest is scholarly. They are primarily directed to those involved in undergraduate and graduate religious studies and programs of formal pastoral formation such as seminaries. We presume that the *basic* questions are good for all levels of inquiry. Realizing that many other questions can be asked, we offer these as models for your use and for you to build upon.

1. Basic Questions

a. What is your understanding of the Catholic Church's teachings on morality?

b. Does your life experience confirm the Church's teaching? Have you had experiences that led you to be challenged by the teachings of the Church concerning objective truth?

c. Are there ways that conflicts between the teachings of the Church on specific issues and an individual's experience can be resolved? Does *Veritatis Splendor* suggest any solutions; does it make any demands?

d. Do the themes of this encyclical (pages 21-23) emerge within homilies, adult education classes, in the media or the reading you have come upon? Are any of these themes new to you? Name them.

e. In what ways would you go about presenting these themes to others?

f. Which teachings emerge as controversial in discussions within church groups, among friends and family members? Why?

g. As you review the document, can you notice any change in the emphasis of the Church on these teachings since you began to study these matters? What explanations can best account for this change in emphasis or for a stress being maintained?

h. Has your understanding of objective truth and moral life changed after reading this document? Why?

i. Why did the Church present this teaching through an encyclical rather than with less authoritative methods?

j. Some may suggest that there no real merit for the *average Catholic* to have a knowledge of this encyclical or of the material within it. Do you agree? What does it mean to be "an average Catholic"?

k. How much about these teachings should be known by the faithful? Should the clergy and religious have a better knowledge of these materials than the average Catholic?

2. Advanced Questions

a. What key elements of the encyclical apply to the pastoral situations you encounter?

b. Does dissent from moral issues affect participation in sacramental life? How?

c. How does your Christian life illustrate the need for moral absolutes? How does it illustrate the presence of these?

d. What elements of your experience resonate with the encyclical's emphasis on: the need for moral absolutes, the definition of human freedom, the understanding of "natural law"?

e. Explain what you understand by the term "natural law." What in your understanding has changed after reading the encyclical?

f. What questions do you need the Church to answer so that you can give assent of mind and heart to the teachings of the encyclical?

g. What experience of the Church and her leadership will be helpful in integrating this teaching into your life?

h. What are the implications of this teaching for your relationships in the following areas: family, work, peers?

i. What is your understanding of the following statements:

Moral reflection is ongoing in development.

Following my conscience....

This is objectively wrong.

Sin.

A subjective norm of morality.

j. What impact does the following statement make upon you?

> *Human frailty, even in the light of God's mercy, is never the basis from which to judge human acts* (n. 104).

How does the statement safeguard your greatest good?

What personal demands does it make of you?

k. What seem to be the "gray areas" of moral actions in the following:

Your life at home

Your life in the workplace

Your financial matters

Your relationships with spouse, family, friends, co-workers, acquaintances, neighbors

Your obligations to the state and nation (local, regional, national, international)?

l. How would this teaching assist you in these areas? How would it assist others?

3. Academic Questions

a. Have historical-critical studies and the "scientific" method helped shape the systems of thinking that assist people in understanding the world and how things relate within it? (Philosophies, psychology, sociology and the physical sciences.) Demonstrate your position with clear references.

b. Are there specific philosophies that stand behind the ethical systems that are challenged by *Veritatis Splendor* ? Can you identify them? Choose one ethical position and show what kind of connection exists there (e.g., causal, correlation?).

c. What does *Veritatis Splendor* propose about the use of "critical" and "scientific" methods? What are the implications for theological inquiry and scholarship? (cf. *VS* 109 ff.)

d. Compare the encyclical with one of the Apostolic Exhortations of Pope John Paul II. [*Catechesi Tradendae: On Catechesis in Our Time* (Mon, Jan. 1, 1979); *Familiaris Consortio: On the Family* (Wed, Dec. 30, 1981); *Reconciliatio et Paenitentia: Reconciliation and Penance* (Sun, Dec. 2, 1984); *Christifidelis Laici: The Vocation and Mission of the Lay Faithful* (Fri, Dec. 30, 1988); *Redemptoris Custos: On the Person and Mission of St. Joseph* (Tue, Aug. 15, 1989)]

Are some themes that are shared among the exhortations present within *Veritatis*? Document your findings.

e. What is the hermeneutic method for exploring this document?

f. How does the encyclical use Scripture?

i) Is Scripture used in a homiletic or exhortatory style, or does it appear intended to provide an in-depth exegesis of the texts?

ii) Does the encyclical reflect any particular school of biblical thought or methodology, e.g. French, German?

Examine the encyclical's citations. What are the sources that Pope John Paul II uses most frequently? Are they surprising? Compare his sources here with his sources in other encyclicals.

g. In this document how is the Marian image of discipleship presented as a model for all Christians?

i) Does John Paul II use this Marian image in other documents?

ii) Does the Pope's appeal to Mary reflect a personal piety, a theological insight or something more than these? Explain.

iii) Do "Petrine" and "Marian" images presented by H.U. Von Balthasar emerge within these teachings? (Confer: *The Office of Peter and The Structure of the Church*. San Francisco: Ignatius Press, ©1986; *The Christian States of Life*. San Francisco: Ignatius Press, © 1983; *The Glory of the Lord: Vol I and II*. San Francisco: Ignatius Press, © 1983, 1984.)

h. What schools of thought, authors and theologians are reflective of this encyclical?

i. Which specific theological trends are being refuted? Which are being promoted? Why?

j. What are the principle objections to this encyclical's teachings? What are their points of convergence? How do they differ?

k. How do other theologians respond to these objections?

l. How should the bishops of this country use this document to present the fullness of this teaching and safeguard authentic Catholic teaching in the following areas: in seminaries, in programs of pastoral formation, in Catholic universities, colleges and schools, from preaching, within religious communities?

m. What are the implications of this teaching for bioethical issues such as reproductive technology and genetic engineering.?

n. Where does it seem that the teachings of this encyclical and technological or scientific methods will converge? Where will they conflict?

o. Select and compare any two commentaries on the encyclical. Be clear in listing their points of agreement and conflict.

p. Using one of the "Key Quotes" provided, or selecting another of your choice, compose an article, write an essay, prepare a sermon or homily to present the teaching behind the citation. Refer to sources outside the encyclical as well, for example, Sacred Scripture, the *Catechism*, the Patristics, etc.

Bibliography

Anderson, David E. "Pope targets threats to traditional Church teaching" in *Religious News Service*, Monday, Oct. 4, 1993.

Arkes, Hadley. "The Splendor of Truth: A Symposium" in *First Things: A Monthly Journal of Religion and Public Life*, Saturday, Jan. 1, 1994, No. 39, pp. 24-30.

Ashley, Benedict. "Does 'The Splendor of Truth' Shine on Bioethics?" in *Ethics and Medics*, Vol. 19, No. 1, Jan. 1994, pp. 3-4.

Briggs, David. "Encyclical-US" in *The Associated Press*, Monday, Oct. 4, 1993, p. 1723.

Burrell, David. "The Splendor of Truth: A Symposium" in *First Things: A Monthly Journal of Religion and Public Life*, Saturday, Jan. 1, 1994, No. 39, pp. 21-23.

Catecismo de la Iglesia Católica. Washington, D.C.: United States Catholic Conference: Coeditores Liturgicos et Alii—Libreria Editrice Vaticana, © 1993.

Catholic News Service. "Encyclical says 'crisis of truth' behind wrong moral theories" in *The AD Times*, Thursday, Oct. 7, 1993, Vol. 5, No. 20, pp. 1-3.

Catholic News Service. "Summary" in *Catholic Trends*, Saturday, Oct. 9, 1993, Vol. 24, No. 6, pp. 1-3.

Comment & Reports. "Catholic theologian rips encyclical" in *The Christian Century*, Wednesday, Nov. 17, 1993, Vol. 110, No. 33, pp. 1153-1154.

Cunningham, Lawrence S. "Veritatis Splendor" in

Commonweal, Friday, Oct. 22, 1993, Vol. CXX, No. 18, pp. 11-12.

Curran, Charles E. "Veritatis Splendor" in *Commonweal*, Friday, Oct. 22, 1993, Vol. CXX, No. 18, p. 14.

Departments: News. "Encyclical stresses obedience" in *The Christian Century*, Saturday, Nov. 20, 1993, Vol. 110, No. 29, pp. 1007-1008.

Doyle, Dennis M. "Veritatis Splendor" in *Commonweal*, Friday, Oct. 22, 1993, Vol. CXX, No. 18, pp. 12-14.

Dulles, Avery. "The Prophetic Humanism of John Paul II" in *America*, Saturday, Oct. 23, 1993, Vol. 169, No. 12, pp. 6-11.

Editorial. "The New Encyclical" in *America*, Saturday, Oct. 23, 1993, Vol. 169, No. 12, p. 3.

Editorial. "Veritatis Splendor" in *Commonweal*, Friday, Oct. 22, 1993, Vol. CXX, No. 18, pp. 3-5.

George, Robert P. "The Splendor of Truth: A Symposium" in *First Things: A Monthly Journal of Religion and Public Life*, Saturday, Jan. 1, 1994, No. 39, pp. 24-30.

Gibeau, Dawn. "Protestants are upbeat about impact of encyclical" in *National Catholic Reporter*, Saturday, Oct. 2, 1993, p. 12.

Häring, Bernard. "Encyclical's one aim: assent and submission" in *National Catholic Reporter*, Friday, Nov. 5, 1993, Vol. 30, No. 3, pp. 15-16.

Hauerwas, Stanley. "The Splendor of Truth: A Symposium" in *First Things: A Monthly Journal of Religion and Public Life*, Saturday, Jan. 1, 1994, No. 39, pp. 21-23.

Hauerwas, Stanley. "Veritatis Splendor" in *Commonweal*, Friday, Oct. 22, 1993, Vol. CXX, No. 18, pp. 16-18.

Hebblethwaite, Peter. "Discipline, not doctrine, is nub of Pope's new encyclical" in *National Catholic Reporter*, Friday, Oct. 1, 1993, Vol. 29, No. 42, p. 9.

Hebblethwaite, Peter. "Church's second millenium often contradicts the first" in *National Catholic Reporter*, Friday, Oct. 15, 1993, pp.15, 17.

Hittinger, Russell. "The Pope and the Theorists" in *Crisis,* Wednesday, Dec. 1, 1993, Vol. 11, No. 11, pp. 31-35.

Hittinger, Russell. "The Splendor of Truth: A Symposium" in

First Things: A Monthly Journal of Religion and Public Life, Saturday, Jan. 1, 1994, No. 39, pp. 16-19.

Jones, L. Gregory. "The Splendor of Truth: A Symposium" in *First Things: A Monthly Journal of Religion and Public Life*, Saturday, Jan. 1, 1994, No. 39, pp. 19-20.

Komonchak, Joseph A. "Veritatis Splendor" in *Commonweal*, Friday, Oct. 22, 1993, Vol. CXX, No. 18, p. 12.

Liptak, David Q. "'Calvin and Hobbes' and Morality" in *The Catholic Transcript*, Friday, Dec. 10, 1993, p. 19.

Liptak, David Q. "Another View of the New Encyclical" in *The Catholic Transcript*, Friday, Oct. 29, 1993, p. 13.

McBrien, Richard P. "Teaching the Truth: John Paul II on moral theology" in *The Christian Century*, Saturday, Nov. 20, 1993, Vol. 110, No. 29, pp. 1004-1005.

McBrien, Richard P. "The Pope's New Encyclical" in *The Catholic Transcript*, Friday, Oct. 29, 1993, p. 12.

McCormick, Richard A. "Veritatis Splendor and Moral Theology" in *America*, Saturday, Oct. 30, 1993, Vol. 169, No. 13, pp. 8-11.

McCormick, Richard. "Document begs many legitimate questions" in *National Catholic Reporter*, Friday, Oct. 15, 1993, p. 17.

McInerny, Ralph. "How to read an encyclical" in *The Catholic Transcript*, Friday, Oct. 29, 1993, p. 12.

McInerny, Ralph. "Locating Right and Wrong" in *Crisis*, Wednesday, Dec. 1, 1993, Vol. 11, No. 11, pp. 37-40.

NCR Staff. "Veritatis Splendor draws cheers and jeers" in *National Catholic Reporter*, Friday, Oct. 15, 1993, p. 15.

Neuhaus, Richard J. "The Truth about Freedom" in *The Wall Street Journal*, Friday, Oct. 8, 1993, pp. A-14.

Neuhaus, Richard J. "The Splendor of Truth: A Symposium" in *First Things: A Monthly Journal of Religion and Public Life*, Saturday, Jan. 1, 1994, No. 39, pp. 14-16.

Neusner, Jacob. "Single Standard of Truth" in *Crisis*, Wednesday, Dec. 1, 1993, Vol. 11, No. 11, pp. 41-43.

Novak, Michael. "Public Arguments: The Hope of Splendor" in *Crisis*, Wednesday, Dec. 1, 1993, Vol. 11, No. 11, pp. 4-8.

O'Connor, John Cardinal. "The Encyclical Is About Freedom" in *Catholic New York*, Thursday, Oct. 7, 1993.

Patrick, Ann E. "Veritatis Splendor" in *Commonweal*, Friday, Oct. 22, 1993, Vol. CXX, No. 18, p. 18.

"Pope-Encyclical: Excerpts" in *The Associated Press*, Tuesday, Oct. 5, 1993, p. 1141.

Pullella, Philip. "Vatican Says Pope's Encyclical is Moral Challenge" in *Reuters*, Tuesday, Oct. 5, 1993, p. 1158.

Ridley, Charles. "Pope's encyclical aims to counter dissidence on morality" in *United Press International*, Tuesday, Oct. 5, 1993, p. 809.

Simpson, Victor L. "Pope-Encyclical" in *The Associated Press*, Tuesday, Oct. 5, 1993, p. 1388.

Scola, Angelo. "Following Christ: On John Paul II's Encyclical 'Veritatis Splendor'" in *Communio*, Winter 1993. Vol XX, No. 4. pp. 724-726.

Smith, Janet E. "Veritatis Splendor" in *Commonweal*, Friday, Oct. 22, 1993, Vol. CXX, No. 18, pp. 14-15.

Sowle Cahill, Lisa. "Veritatis Splendor" in *Commonweal*, Friday, Oct. 22, 1993, Vol. CXX, No. 18, pp. 15-16.

Steinfels, Peter. "Papal Encyclical Says Church Must Enforce Basic Morality" in *New York Times*, Sunday, Oct. 3, 1993, pp. 1-26.

Wilson, James Q. "'Calvin & Hobbes' and John Paul" in *New York Times*, Friday, Nov. 26, 1993, p. A35.

Suggested Additional Bibliography

Ashley, B.H. "What is moral theology? Part II" in *Medics and Ethics*, August 1993. Vol. 18, 8, p. 3.

Caffara, Carlo. *Living in Christ*. San Francisco: Ignatius Press, © 1987.

Carlen, IHM, Sr. Claudia. *The Papal Encyclicals*, Vols. 1-5. Ann Arbor, MI: The Pieran Press, © 1990.

The *Catechism of the Catholic Church*. Boston: St. Paul Books & Media, © Libreria Editrice Vaticana, 1994.

Catéchism de l'Église Catholique. Ottawa, Canada: Concacan Inc. pour Libreria Editrice Vaticana, © 1993.

Latin Text. Citta del Vaticano: Libreria Editrice Vaticana, © 1992.

Charles, SJ, Rodger. *The Social Teaching of Vatican II*, 2nd ed. San Francisco: Ignatius Press, © 1988.

Dulles, A. *The Reshaping of Catholicism, Current challenges in the theology of the Church.* San Francisco. Harper and Row, © 1988.

Finnis, John. *Natural Law, Natural Rights*. Oxford, UK: Clarendon Press, © 1980.

Finnis, John. *Moral Absolutes: Tradition, Revision and Truth*. Washington, D.C.: Catholic University of America Press, © 1991.

Grisez, G. *Living a Christian Life*. Chicago: Franciscan Press, © 1993.

Grisez, G. *The Way of the Lord Jesus*, Vol 1. Christian Morality Chicago: Franciscan Press, © 1983.

John Paul II. *The Splendor of Truth.* Boston: St. Paul Books & Media, 1993.

May, W. E. *An Introduction to Moral Theology*. Huntington, IN: Our Sunday Visitor, © 1991.

Mulligan, STL, James J. *Theologians and Authority Within the Living Church*. Braintree, MA: The Pope John XXIII Medical-Moral Research and Education Center, © 1986.

Ratzinger, Joseph Cardinal. *Principles of Catholic Morality*. San Francisco: Ignatius Press, © 1992.

Ratzinger, Joseph Cardinal. "The Catechism of the Catholic Church and the optimism of the redeemed" in *Communio* (20) Fall, 1993, pp. 469-484.

Rice, Charles. *Fifty Questions on the Natural Law: What It Is and Why We Need It.* San Francisco: Ignatius Press, © 1993.

Schmaus, M. *Dogma 4, the Church, Its Origin and Structure*. New York: Sheed and Ward, © 1972.

Sullivan, SJ, F.A. *The Church We Believe in, One, Holy, Catholic, and Apostolic*. Mahwah, NJ: Paulist Press, © 1988.

Tavard, G. H. *The Church, Community of Salvation, an Ecumenical Ecclesiology*. Collegeville, MN: The Liturgical Press, © 1993.

St. Paul Book & Media Centers

ALASKA
750 West 5th Ave., Anchorage, AK 99501; 907-272-8183

CALIFORNIA
3908 Sepulveda Blvd., Culver City, CA 90230; 310-397-8676
5945 Balboa Ave., San Diego, CA 92111; 619-565-9181
46 Geary Street, San Francisco, CA 94108; 415-781-5180

FLORIDA
145 S.W. 107th Ave., Miami, FL 33174; 305-559-6715

HAWAII
1143 Bishop Street, Honolulu, HI 96813; 808-521-2731

ILLINOIS
172 North Michigan Ave., Chicago, IL 60601; 312-346-4228

LOUISIANA
4403 Veterans Memorial Blvd., Metairie, LA 70006; 504-887-7631

MASSACHUSETTS
50 St. Paul's Ave., Jamaica Plain, Boston, MA 02130; 617-522-8911
Rte. 1, 885 Providence Hwy., Dedham, MA 02026; 617-326-5385

MISSOURI
9804 Watson Rd., St. Louis, MO 63126; 314-965-3512

NEW JERSEY
561 U.S. Route 1, Wick Plaza, Edison, NJ 08817; 908-572-1200

NEW YORK
150 East 52nd Street, New York, NY 10022; 212-754-1110
78 Fort Place, Staten Island, NY 10301; 718-447-5071

OHIO
2105 Ontario Street, Cleveland, OH 44115; 216-621-9427

PENNSYLVANIA
214 W. DeKalb Pike, King of Prussia, PA 19406; 610-337-1882

SOUTH CAROLINA
243 King Street, Charleston, SC 29401; 803-577-0175

TENNESSEE
4811 Poplar Ave., Memphis, TN 38117; 901-761-0874

TEXAS
114 Main Plaza, San Antonio, TX 78205; 210-224-8101

VIRGINIA
1025 King Street, Alexandria, VA 22314; 703-549-3806

GUAM
285 Farenholt Avenue, Suite 308, Tamuning, Guam 96911; 671-646-7745

CANADA
3022 Dufferin Street, Toronto, Ontario, Canada M6B 3T5; 416-781-9131